D1001045

WEREWOLVES DO WORD PROBLEMS!

BY THERESE M. SHEA

Gareth Stevens
PUBLISHING

Please visit our website, www.garethstevens.com. For a free color catalog of all our high-quality books, call toll free 1-800-542-2595 or fax 1-877-542-2596.

Cataloging-in-Publication Data

Names: Shea, Therese M.
Title: Werewolves do word problems! / Therese M. Shea.
Description: New York : Gareth Stevens Publishing, 2019. | Series: Monsters do math! | Includes glossary and index.
Identifiers: ISBN 9781538233023 (pbk.) | ISBN 9781538229361 (library bound) | ISBN 9781538233030 (6 pack)
Subjects: LCSH: Problem solving--Juvenile literature. | Word problems (Mathematics)--Juvenile literature. | Werewolves--Juvenile literature.
Classification: LCC QA63.S54 2019 | DDC 510.76--dc23

First Edition

Published in 2019 by
Gareth Stevens Publishing
111 East 14th Street, Suite 349
New York, NY 10003

Designer: Sarah Liddell
Editor: Kate Light
Illustrator: Bobby Griffiths

Photo credits: p. 4 Denis Andricic/Shutterstock.com; p. 5 Sunset Boulevard/Contributor/Corbis Historical/Getty Images; p. 6 AdamBMorgan/Wikimedia Commons; p. 8 Pi-Lens/Shutterstock.com; p. 10 NAAN/Shutterstock.com; p. 12 guentermanaus/Shutterstock.com; p. 14 Scanraill/Shutterstock.com; p. 16 Jef Wodniack/Shutterstock.com; p. 19 We hope/Wikimedia Commons; p. 20 Steve McAlister/Photolibrary/Getty Images; p. 21 ortlemma/Shutterstock.com.

Printed in the United States of America

CPSIA compliance information: Batch #CW19GS: For further information contact Gareth Stevens, New York, New York at 1-800-542-2595.

CONTENTS

Worried About Werewolves? . . 4

A Math Story 6

Look for Clues 8

Searching for Answers 16

Double Trouble! 18

Not-All-Bad Biters 20

Glossary 22

Answer Key 22

For More Information 23

Index 24

Words in the glossary appear in **bold** type the first time they are used in the text.

There's a full moon in the sky. Some say the full moon means werewolves will be on the hunt. A werewolf is a person who turns into a wolf at night and back into a person during the day. A hungry werewolf hunts for anything—or anyone—that looks tasty!

Are you worried? You shouldn't be. The werewolves in this book like to munch on numbers more than people! They'll help you understand and **solve** word problems. Check your work with the answer key on page 22.

THE WORD "WEREWOLF" COMES FROM OLD ENGLISH
WORDS THAT MEAN "MAN-WOLF."

A MATH STORY

Many stories feature werewolves as scary monsters. Word problems are just like stories, but with math! The most important **strategy** for solving word problems is to read carefully. Then, use facts you find to set up and solve an **equation**.

MONSTER FACTS!
IT'S SAID THAT PEOPLE HAVE NO MEMORY OF THE THINGS THEY DO AS WEREWOLVES!

One night, a werewolf bit 15 people. On a second night, it bit 5 people. How many people did it bite altogether?

Your equation should look like this:

15 people + 5 people = ? people

Do you want to know if there are werewolves where you live? Look for clues like paw prints!

You can find clue words in word problems to find out if you should add. Here are some common addition words:

add	in all
altogether	sum
both	total

MONSTER FACTS!

SOME PEOPLE ARE SAID TO TURN INTO WEREWOLVES BECAUSE THEIR PARENTS ARE WEREWOLVES!

Twelve werewolves were seen in a town and 3 were found in the forest. How many werewolves were spotted in all?

The words "in all" are your clue to add. Use the picture to help you fill in and solve the equation below.

? werewolves + ? werewolves = ? werewolves

Here are some common subtraction words to look for in word problems:

fewer than   less than
difference   left
how many more   how much less
remain

MONSTER FACTS!
SOME PEOPLE THINK HUMANS CHANGE INTO WEREWOLVES DURING A FULL MOON. OTHERS THINK WEREWOLVES CHANGE WHEN THEY WANT TO!

Imagine 20 werewolves were out on a night with a full moon. As the sun rose, 10 werewolves turned back into people. How many werewolves remained?

The word "remained" tells us to subtract. Set up and solve a subtraction equation to answer the question. Use the picture to help you.

You have a problem if the werewolves where you live are multiplying. That means their numbers are growing fast!

The words "double," "times," and "twice" are clues in word problems that tell you to multiply.

MONSTER FACTS!
SOME SAY THE PLANT WOLFSBANE COULD BE USED TO KEEP WEREWOLVES AWAY. IT'S ACTUALLY A POISONOUS PLANT YOU SHOULD NEVER TOUCH!

Nine werewolves were scaring the people in a town. By the next full moon, the town had 3 times as many werewolves! How many werewolves did they have?

The picture below will help you solve this equation:

9 werewolves x 3 = ? werewolves

13

If you can't get your werewolf problem under control, you might need to call in some monster hunters! They'll **divide** the werewolves into equal groups so they're easier to control.

Some words that tell you to use division in word problems are "each," "per," and "equal."

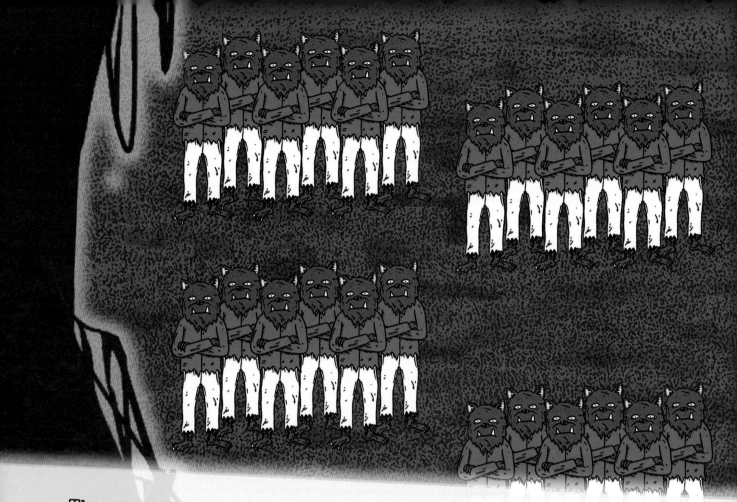

There are 24 werewolves in the woods and 4 monster hunters. If the hunters divide the werewolves into 4 equal groups, how many werewolves are in each group?

Use the picture to help you solve the equation. Remember, you can always draw your own picture to help you understand any word problem!

24 werewolves ÷ 4 hunters = ? werewolves in each group

Searching for werewolves isn't easy. You have to hunt them at night. They might not be where you expect them to be!

Sometimes the number you're trying to find to answer a word problem isn't at the end of the equation!

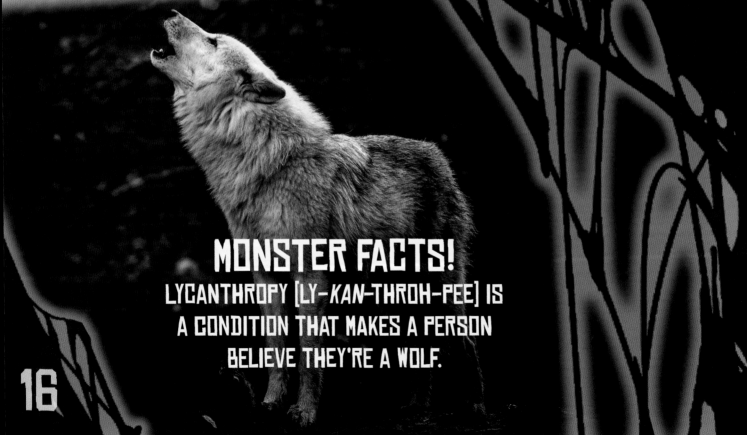

MONSTER FACTS!
LYCANTHROPY [LY-*KAN*-THROH-PEE] IS A CONDITION THAT MAKES A PERSON BELIEVE THEY'RE A WOLF.

A monster hunter captures some werewolves one night. Three escape the next night. If she captured 30 werewolves in all, how many did she capture the first night?

? werewolves − 3 werewolves = 30 werewolves

Even though you should set up a subtraction equation for this word problem, you'll add 3 and 30 to find the answer.

Some people say werewolves turn into vampires after death. That's twice as many terrible monsters to face! To solve some word problems, you need to take two or more steps to find the final answer. In fact, you may need to use more than one math **operation.**

MONSTER FACTS!
WOLVES AREN'T COMMON IN SOME COUNTRIES. THOSE PLACES HAVE TALES OF PEOPLE WHO TAKE THE FORM OF TIGERS, BEARS, OR EVEN **HYENAS!**

There were 9 werewolves on the hunt. Then, some vampires joined them. Then, 6 more werewolves showed up. If there were 20 monsters in all, how many vampires joined them?

9 werewolves + ? vampires + 6 werewolves = 20 monsters

THERE ARE A FEW WAYS TO SOLVE THIS. TRY ADDING THE NUMBER OF WEREWOLVES AND THEN SUBTRACTING YOUR ANSWER FROM THE TOTAL NUMBER OF MONSTERS.

NOT-ALL-BAD BITERS

You may not want to get too close to a werewolf. Don't forget! A bite could turn you into a werewolf yourself! However, these hairy monsters do make solving word problems a bit more fun.

If the werewolves in this book have helped you understand word problems, then they're not all bad. Just remember, the most important part of solving word problems is reading carefully. Then, decide which operation to use and set up your equation. Draw some pictures of werewolves if it helps!

REAL WOLVES LIVE WITH THEIR FAMILIES IN GROUPS CALLED PACKS. IS THERE A PACK OF WEREWOLVES LIVING NEAR YOU?

21

GLOSSARY

bullet: a small piece of metal that is shot out of a gun

divide: to break up

equation: in math, a statement that two values are equal

hyena: a meat-eating animal that looks much like a dog and lives in Africa and southern Asia

operation: a mathematical process (such as addition or multiplication) that is used for getting one number or set of numbers from others according to a rule

poisonous: having poison, which is something that causes illness or death

solve: to find the answer

strategy: a carefully thought-out plan

ANSWER KEY

page 7: 20 people

page 9: 12 werewolves + 3 werewolves = 15 werewolves

page 11: 20 werewolves - 10 werewolves = 10 werewolves

page 13: 27 werewolves

page 15: 6 werewolves in each group

page 17: 33 werewolves

page 19: 5 vampires

FOR MORE INFORMATION

BOOKS

Bullard, Lisa. *I'm Fearsome and Furry! Meet a Werewolf.* Minneapolis, MN: Millbrook Press, 2015.

Markovics, Joyce. *All about Word Problems.* Vero Beach, FL: Rourke Educational Media, 2013.

Williams, Zella, and Rebecca Wingard-Nelson. *Word Problems Using Addition and Subtraction.* New York, NY: Enslow Publishing, 2017.

WEBSITES

A Collection of Math Word Problems for Grades 1 to 6
www.mathplayground.com/wpdatabase/wpindex.html
Quiz yourself on this site.

Word Problems
www.ixl.com/math/word-problems
Test your word-problem skills!

INDEX

common addition
    words 8

common division
    words 14

common multiplication
    words 12

common subtraction
    words 10

equations 6, 7, 9, 11,
    13, 15, 16, 17, 20

lycanthropy 16

math operations 18, 20

monster hunters 14, 15,
    17

moon 4, 10, 11, 13

packs 21

parents 8

paw prints 8

silver bullets 14

vampires 18, 19

wolfsbane 12

wolves 4, 16, 21